If you know you have the means to afford a home for you and your family and have been denied traditional financing, do yourself a big favor and read this book.

Or, if you are pretty sure you can afford a home, but you have been too afraid to ask or don't know where to begin, this book ceretainly can help ~~get you started~~ in the right direction.

~~of the things~~ ~~about is teaching~~ ~~how~~ to own their own home – even when they've been rejected by the big banks. I was born in Vietnam and I have a strong will for success and creating win-wins in life. I rarely take no for an answer, and it is my privilege to show you how you can create your success, too, regardless of your current circumstances.

Buy Your Dream Home
ALL BUYERS QUALIFY ✓

BY
TIL LOWERY

TL GLOBAL
APPLIED KNOWLEDGE IS POWER

ISBN--13: 978-1-944913-68-7

INTRODUCTION

One of the best ways to start accumulating wealth is to own your own home. That's why home ownership has been referred to as the American Dream. Unfortunately, the American Dream isn't always available to everyone who lives in America.

Sometimes, you don't have the required two-year work history, or you are self-employed, or you're too new to America to qualify for a regular home loan. Or maybe you've had a credit blip due to unforeseen circumstances. What then?

I have been a real estate agent and broker since 1990. I've assisted hundreds, maybe even thousands, of people to achieve the American Dream of home ownership, and one of the most frustrating parts of the process is home financing. It has always been hard for me to find out that a good family with decent income has given up on their dream of owning their own home just because they can't get traditional financing.

Several years ago, when a relative of mine couldn't qualify for a loan, I tried something few have even heard of let alone considered – I bought the house in my name using my credit and allowed him to make all the payments directly to me. There was no question in my mind that he could afford to make the monthly payment. I trusted him. Thus, I was merely doing what I thought was the right thing to do. I had no interest in getting a commission or making a huge profit. It made me feel good to help.

I didn't think much about it until a friend and business partner of mine approached me about helping another person in the same way. Again, I did it without hesitation, not realizing just how many people are in a similar situation. Their income may totally justify the purchase, but for whatever reason, they cannot meet the bank's requirements for getting a traditional loan.

Now, don't go to a "loan shark" and get outrageous terms where you could eventually be forced out of the house due to a balloon payment. I'm talking about having a traditional type of mortgage from a private-party lender with payments you can afford and no balloon payments just like traditional financing.

Buying your home should not be an act of desperation, but a joyful, fulfilling experience that you feel confident about. When you own your own home, you get to take advantage of appreciation (the value of your home increasing) and yet still pay the same mortgage month after month (maybe a little more if taxes and insurance go up in your area.)

If you don't own your own home, you end up paying rent. Rent continues to rise and it is your landlord who receives the benefit of the real estate appreciation, plus increased monthly income from the rental market going up, too!

When you own your own home, you benefit from special tax credits for mortgage interest that is not available to you as a renter.

Have you been trying to buy a home, but you always get stopped when they check your credit? Are you feeling crushed by the difficulties of financing? If you could qualify, would you opt to be a homeowner?

If you are hearing a "yes" in your head to these questions, you already know it would be nice to have a place you can call your own – a place to decorate or remodel any way you want, a place to raise your children and make memories, have friends over, or plant a garden.

There are so many more benefits to home ownership than just building wealth. That is why owning your own home can be so important.

I mentor people who don't qualify for traditional financing and connect them with resources they can use to get the home of their dreams. I've been doing this since 2006. If you believe I can help you in any way, please feel free to reach out to me. I'm committed to your success.

At the end of each chapter, you will find a questionnaire that you can fill out directly in the book or you may want to use as a notepad to write your answers, thoughts, and actions. There's no test, and no one's ever going to ask to see it. It's just to help you follow along as you learn something new.

In the meantime, you can check out:

Til Lowery
TL Global
www.ShopOwnerFinance.com

Top Reasons People Choose to Purchase Their Own Home:

1. They want independence.
2. They want the tax breaks that come with home ownership.
3. They are tired of wasting their money on rent.
4. They want to raise their kids and build memories in their own home.
5. They want something they can leave to their children.
6. They want to build equity over time.
7. They are fully responsible and know how to care for a home.
8. They know that they are wasting valuable time – a nonrenewable resource – by waiting.

"You Can Have Everything in Life You Want, if You Will Just Help Enough Other People Get What They Want." - -Zig Ziglar

CHAPTER 1

REJECTED! YOU ARE NOT ALONE

After helping those first two people in 2006, I was busy and didn't think much about helping more people with credit challenges. It was when I continued to see more and more clients not qualifying for traditional mortgages, that the idea to provide private-lender financing was born.

It didn't seem fair to me that good people with decent income couldn't get traditional financing. Over time, I began to realize how many people needed to learn about alternative, safe, legal, and guaranteed ways to fund purchasing their home.

9

There are so many reasons good people get rejected for a home loan. Here are just some of the problems I've seen and been able to help with:

1. **Tax Returns**

   Banks want to see at least two years of properly filed tax returns with stable income.

2. **Divorce**

   Not only are divorces painful emotionally, they also come with steep financial losses and credit disruption for both parties.

3. **Bankruptcy**

   Bankruptcy can significantly lower your credit score and affect your ability to qualify for a mortgage for seven to ten years.

4. **Foreclosure**

   Credit companies start reporting foreclosure on your credit report as soon as you are 30 days late, and it can take up to <u>seven years</u> to go off your credit report.

5. **Self-employed**
   Self-employed people and business owners are the backbone of the U.S. economy and yet, they get the short end of the stick because they are seen as risky borrowers.

6. **Non-verifiable Income**
   Without a "guaranteed" form of income like W2 paystubs or consistent direct deposits, many buyers, such as contractors, have trouble proving a steady source of income.

7. **Student Loan Defaults**
   A default on a student loan causes an uphill battle when it comes to lenders as they often have an exaggerated effect on your credit.

8. **Medical Bills**

   Medical bills destroy people's credit more than any other reason.

9. **Tax Lien or Judgement**

   A tax lien can make it difficult for a lender to approve your loan.

10. **Employment Gap** You might be in between jobs, but a high wage earner. Many lenders require a consistent two-year employment history.

The list goes on including general credit challenges, non-citizenship status, foreign national status, lack of work documents, having a previous short sale, or even having perfect credit but wanting to save it for something else.

When people get tired of being denied, they come to me to look for financing alternatives.

I first want to know if working with me will be a good fit for you and can we provide a financially sound solution for your specific situation.

I have had a few cases where people sought my mentoring services and wanted to work with me, but we were not the best solution for them. When I assessed their financial situation and realized that they could get a similar type of loan at a lower interest rate than they could from my immediate resources, I had to point them to our referral network.

Why? Because it is the only right thing to do. We always take care of our customers first.

Vetting homebuyers has become somewhat of a specialty for me. I don't put clients through rigorous screening, wanting to know everything about their lives like their social security number and their dog's name. I really just want to know that I am dealing with normal and honest human beings. I know that if I don't serve my clients and associates with integrity, I will be undermining my own purpose and success. So, I don't do it.

By now, you're probably asking yourself, "How does this work? Do I really own my home or does someone else? If I'm not borrowing from a bank, how do I know it's legit?"

You're not alone, and you should ask serious questions about legitimacy before you ever make a big decision such as buying a home.

At the end of each chapter, you'll find a simple self-assessment questionnaire that you can fill out to evaluate your own situation. That's just for you to navigate the waters and see if you're ready to explore further. If you've been looking and everyone has been rejecting you, you're not the first to hit this wall. You've found the right place.

Chapter 1:
Self-Evaluation Questionnaire

1. What made you pick up this book? What's your situation?

2. Have you ever had troubles buying a home because of any of the problems listed on pages 9-11, such as bad credit following a divorce? If so, which one(s)?

3. You've likely heard of owner financing (a seller carrying a loan for the buyer). Can you think of reasons why a seller would or wouldn't want to carry a loan?

If an owner needs to move quickly and sell their home, they might be open to carrying back the loan, knowing that they can always repossess it and sell it to someone else if you default. Do you see possible risks for the seller that make it tricky to find the ones who are willing to carry?

Do you have personal experience working with a private lender instead of a bank? If so, what was your experience and what did you learn?

TAKING A CALCULATED RISK

When I was a small girl, my dad had the courage to take a calculated risk. We could have either lived indefinitely under a corrupt and failing society, or risk everything in search of a better life. We didn't have much to lose.

My family and I were living in a war-torn Vietnam where people didn't have enough clothing, food, or shelter. To make things worse, it was also a dictatorship. The army had blanket power to shoot and kill for any reason.

Because of all this, my dad devised a master plan and plotted our escape. He took two full years to build a boat by hand and then went fishing every day to convince harbor guards that he was a fisherman by trade. From time to time, he would throw them his best catch for the day as a gift to win their favor.

In the beginning, the guards would search every inch of his boat on the way out to sea and on the way back into the harbor. Over the two years, they came to trust him and simply waved him in and out of the harbor.

The night of our escape, we loaded three generations (forty-six relatives in all), into the hull of this little boat. We were told not to make a sound – not even to talk to each other. How the adults got the little ones not to cry, I'll never know.

When morning came, my dad sailed out to sea, and the guards waved him out. We never came back. My dad planned enough food and water for four days, but we lost our sense of direction during a storm and totally ran out of supplies. When it rained, we collected what water we could using our T-shirts and rung them out to drink.

Within a few days, my dad was too weak from hunger to start the outboard motor. Fortunately, my older brother was still in shape to do it. When even my brother couldn't start the motor, we floated, delirious from lack of food and water. We never knew where we would land, or if we would land.

The trip lasted sixteen days.

Thanks to that experience, many things that are seen as risky to others, appear more like opportunities to me. This experience contributed to my mentality to take chances and develop new ways of doing things instead of fearing the unknown. My dad taught me to have the courage to take action with the faith of knowing that I will eventually find a way with hard work and determination. Being afraid seems to trap you in square one.

My dad had the courage to make a calculated risk and the patience to do whatever was necessary to create a better future for us. Even though things went wrong along the way, we eventually found refuge in the United States of America where we went on to pursue the American Dream.

Back in Vietnam, our whole family lived in a shack the size of an American bedroom – without air conditioning or any luxury. When we moved to America and moved into our first home, it was small and cluttered, but we were tickled to death with pride to even have such a home.

It was always kept immaculate. I remember cleaning the toilets for my family and doing all the household chores, happy that I simply had a house I could clean.

Today, I take people through the third-party owner financing program and explain from A-Z how it's done. Each time, I get a reminder of the warm feeling I had when our family first acquired our very own home.

I know my dad is looking down from heaven, proud of his bold decision and courage. From a hopeless reality in which we feared for our lives, we went on to have a successful family of doctors, dentists, pharmacists, optometrists, business owners, and real estate professionals. I am forever grateful to my dad for having the courage it took to provide us with an environment we could succeed in.

America has been good to me, and I've always wanted to give back. To me, providing an opportunity for others to experience their dream of home ownership when they would otherwise never qualify to get a loan is my way of giving back.

CHAPTER 2

GOING AROUND THE BIG BANKS

I know you are wondering how a homebuyer could go about getting a loan with no credit check. And, if that is the case, how can you possibly do it?

Here's the secret: Don't get your loan from a bank.

Going around the bank is ideal if you have the income to afford your monthly payment and a down payment saved but lack credit or some of the other stringent requirements for a traditional loan. The solution is to purchase your home with owner financing, but not from just *any* owner.

You may have heard that if you find the right motivated seller, you might be able to purchase the home from them on a contract for deed. One thing to consider is that when a homeowner puts their home up for sale, they are motivated to find a buyer who can purchase the home, not carry a loan for them. When you scour MLS listings, scan newspaper ads, look online, or drive around neighborhoods looking for "For Sale" signs, you'll find homes for sale, but you won't know exactly why they are selling. Even if the owner gives a reason for the sale of the home, there may be more behind the story.

The owner/seller normally wants to get cashed out right away. For example, the seller may have inherited a house that they didn't want and may be overwhelmed with the costs it takes to keep the property. Other times, they may have lost their job and can no longer afford to pay the monthly mortgage, leaving them in a high-pressure situation. Once their grown-up children move out of the house, they may just want to take a year off for travel and need the money from the home sale to do so.

When you approach a seller, you have no idea what's behind the sale. And, they rarely give you the reason.

If you're trying to get a loan by going around the banks, owner financing is a terrific option; however, here are some issues you might run into if you're trying to convince a *specific* seller to owner finance you their home:

1. Most owners don't want to carry the loan! They don't know you and they don't want to take the risk. Looking for that special owner out of dozens of possible homes can be almost impossible.

2. You might find an owner who will carry the loan, but it might not be the right house! After all that trouble, you should at least get a house that fits your needs.

3. If the seller is desperate to sell the house with owner financing, it might be because it is overpriced or in poor condition.

4. Unless you are a lawyer, you are taking a risk trying to create all the forms you need to safeguard yourself. Even then, getting legal protection with owner financing is a highly specialized skill.

5. You'll have to take care of getting the sale recorded, figuring out the contingencies, amortizing the loan, keeping accurate records of your payments, making sure your money gets to the underlying lender, tracking down the owner if they move, changing banks, and more. Remember, the sellers are probably amateurs, too.

6. You'll have a relationship with that seller for many years to come. What if they're not that easy to get along with?

7. There is a myriad of pitfalls you've got to plan for in advance – and you won't know what they are unless you've had a lot of experience with this.

After helping a few people, I began to realize how many things could go wrong. I literally paid one person's mortgage for several months so that the bank wouldn't foreclose. I went in the red on the deal, not just because I cared for them, but also because it was my good credit at stake!

I realized that if people are going to buy on behalf of others in this way, they need to be protected from the anticipated ups and downs in life, as well as the unanticipated.

That's when I decided that for everything to work in a win-win fashion sustainably, everyone involved in the process has to be educated on the end-to-end process with full transparency. Every party has to be trained on what to do, what to expect, and be guided every step of the way. Ultimately, they need to understand all the upsides as well as worst case scenarios.

I charge a fee to educate people, but only to those who are ready and understand our process completely. Then, I guide you through the financing program because no one else in the real estate industry knows exactly how I do it. If the plan resonates with you and feels right with you, you'll know it.

All parties in the deal need training, and I have worked with my attorneys to nail everything down right so I can take care of everyone.

After many years of working with the core idea, trying different ideas, testing the results, brainstorming, and learning from successes and mistakes, I developed something unique:

We call it third-party owner financing: owner financing with no credit check on any home you want!

("Third-party owner financing" was originally coined by our senior trainer, Richard Whitmore, who has been in this business over thirty years.)

To bring my idea into full reality, I formed everything from scratch: a legal team, new partners, documents, legal processes, entities, and protections for all parties involved. I improved on this idea for over ten years. Even after developing the idea and the core machinery to back it up, I realized that teaching the people involved how to do it was the main thing standing in the way of everyone getting the outcome they wanted. At that point, I created TL Global, a training business to help many people orchestrate these types of deals.

I have discovered that mentoring is the key to all of it. Without providing guidance for everyone involved in the process, all my hard work in the development phase of this idea might have gone completely to waste.

Now, the infrastructure is in place, and I simply mentor people to assure everything happens seamlessly. Here are three things I do that makes a huge difference for a homebuyer:

1. Teach everyone involved what they need to know to make a deal that works for everybody.
2. Provide a network of people who are skilled in third-party owner financing to take the pressure off all parties involved.
3. Provide a proven legal framework for all parties so everyone is protected.

At this point, I've helped hundreds of families buy their homes even though they couldn't get traditional financing. And, I have to say, "It feels good."

Chapter 2:
Self-Evaluation Questionnaire

We've talked about getting owner financing as the best way of getting a loan when a bank won't give you one. How much time would you be able to spend looking for that one owner open to carrying the loan?

Do you think it would it be helpful to have a friend connect you to an ethical private lender who could give you a loan?

It's definitely best to have the seller carry the loan if you can't get a bank loan. The trouble with relying on the seller is that you might not like the particular home they are selling. Would it be a relief to have the loan lined up through a private party before you started looking?

We've talked about why the seller might find it risky to carry a loan. By the same token, there is a certain amount of risk involved in borrowing from a private lender. Consider the safeguards you might need folded into the loan documents to protect yourself. List a few ideas of what you'd like to include in the contract.

Would you appreciate the freedom to be able to pick out your own home even if the current seller doesn't want to carry the loan?

CHAPTER 3

THE BEST WAY TO GET A PRIVATE LOAN

I have discovered the awesome key to owner financing. <u>Don't use the seller for the financing.</u>

I know. It sounds weird. And, like I already told you, most sellers don't want to carry the loan. They want all their money in cash so they can move on with their lives. They don't want a long-term relationship with you. They've got lives of their own.

Of course, if you can qualify for a loan with the bank, the seller will be cashed out and you will be benefitting from the best terms and interest rates. In that case, you wouldn't need the TL Global system.

With TL Global, you normally find out upon initial contact if our system is right for you. And, if we believe you can qualify for a conventional loan, we can help by referring you to an amazing network of highly efficient loan officers we trust. Most of the time when we sit down to help a client, they have already been denied a home loan.

If we agree we are a fit to work together and you've received your training, the process starts with shopping for a home. Just like with a conventional loan pre-approval letter, you get to choose the home you want. Then, I step in and help to get that home without going through a bank by using the TL Global system – and I've become an expert at doing it.

Here's what you need to know when you're picking out your home:

1. It can be any home you choose. I can't choose it for you.
2. It can be new, old, city, country, one story, two story, whatever you want.
3. You don't need income verification.
4. You don't need tax returns.
5. You don't need to get your credit run.
6. You pick any house in any price range you can afford.
7. You work with a realtor to pick out the home and decide how much to offer the seller.

You call all the shots: the due diligence, the negotiation via your realtor, the inspections, etc. This is going to be your home. You don't want to overpay, and your lender doesn't want you to overpay either.

By now, you're probably asking yourself, "Is this for real? What is third-party owner financing?"

Here are a few other questions you probably have:

1. Is the title in my name?
2. What is the interest rate?
3. What are the payments?
4. Who are these people?
5. How long have they been in business?
6. How do I know that this isn't a scam?

I'm glad you asked.

1. Yes, you get a deed in your name, and it is recorded in the county courthouse where you buy the home.
2. The interest rate is going to be higher than what you'd normally get if you had great credit.
3. The payment depends on what kind of house you want, what price you've negotiated with the

seller, how much you put down, what your interest rate is, how much insurance costs, and the property taxes in the area. It's your house, and you decide on what size, neighborhood, condition, and price.

4. You'll meet my associates and me in person and get to know us.

5. We've been doing this since 2006.

6. If you're afraid it's a scam or just something you're not interested in, I'll be glad to make friends with you, but there's no sales pitch or pressure to proceed. This is one of the biggest purchases you're likely to make in your life. There isn't anyone in a better position than you to know whether the program will work for you. You will receive full transparency and full disclosure because that's the only way to do business.

When I interview people, it's to make sure we're a good fit. That's why I'm kind of antique-y about meeting the people I work with in person. By the time you're done reading this book, you'll know most of the process, if not all of it. And, I do have a website at www.shopownerfinance.com where you can see me talking about it in further detail.

It's not only important that you understand everything, but also that you meet with us face-to-face so you can evaluate for yourself if this is the right system for you and if you're ready to work with us.

We do everything in person and one family at a time. Each family needs individual attention. People from all over the world come to meet with us. Soon, we will have centers in Georgia, Arizona, and other states, but for now, people come to our location in Houston, Texas.

Chapter 3:
Self-Evaluation Questionnaire

Can you see the benefits of having your financing lined up before going into escrow? What happens if you're in escrow but your loan falls through?

Are you savvy enough to do your due diligence during escrow, getting your prospective home inspected to make sure everything's sound?

If you're prequalified, you can choose any house you like as long as you can afford it. If you've put some thought into the kind of home you like and you see it, you can put in an offer right away. What kind of home would be your first choice?

You probably realize that certain protections have to be built into any contract. Are you okay with traveling to meet a professional to verify trustworthiness and determine if they are a good fit for you?

CHAPTER 4

THIRD-PARTY OWNER FINANCING

Now, it's time to explain the most important thing you need to know –third-party owner financing. What is it and how does it work?

Remember how I told you that the best way to get a loan without a bank is to get owner financing? And remember how I told you that there are a lot of pitfalls to finding the right owner among dozens of listings and convincing them to carry your loan for 30 years? On top of that, I explained how you must figure out all the legal details to boot!

42

Well, it's finally time to explain "third-party owner financing" in more detail.

What is third-party owner financing?

This is a process in which you enter into a legal agreement with a private party to finance the home you want. You identify the home you want and work out the price. Since most sellers don't want to finance a perfect stranger, I

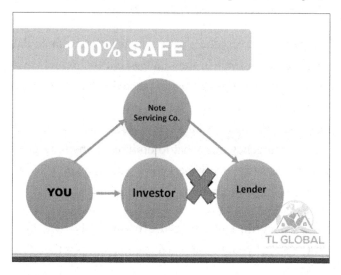

arrange for an investor with good credit to buy your home from the seller and sell it to you upon closing. This is prearranged in writing, so you are assured ownership.

You get the home recorded in your name. You pay off the mortgage over time, just as you would to a bank. The only difference is that the "third-party owner" is an individual instead of a bank. Typically, we set up for you to pay to a note servicing company that you select.

To make sure everyone's safe, all parties are trained the same way each time so they understand the process and can support you. I put a trust in place that clearly defines everybody's role so there are no secrets or misunderstandings. Additionally, the trust spells out every contingency and what to do in case anything goes wrong. That way, everyone knows what to expect and is protected in case something unexpected happens.

It's a wonderful synergy, and everyone gets what they want. You get your house, the title company gets their fee, the realtor gets a commission, and the third-party owner-investor gets a monthly payment from a reliable person.

What Safeguards Do You Have?

When you've done something for as long as I have, you run into just about every situation that could happen. For example, what if someone in the agreement dies? Misses a payment? Changes their mind? Everything has been thought of and dealt with over the years.

Even if something completely unforeseen happens, there is a clause for that, too. Real estate and financing have been in existence for thousands of years, and we've been able to find solutions that work for each and every party involved. Over several decades of research, testing, and experience, I've seen just about every imaginable and unimaginable problem in the realm of third-party owner financing.

My company, TL Global, gets paid for teaching and connecting. We make sure you're a good fit for this program, that you get protected legally, and you have the professional resources you need. TL Global is not a real estate company or brokerage. It has no interest in the properties; TL Global does training only.

How Does This Work?

The process is fast and easy for you if you're a good fit. Essentially, that means you can afford to buy a home, but you just haven't been able to qualify for a traditional bank loan. TL Global takes that problem out of your hands.

Here are the steps:

1. You arrange for a live meeting to see if TL Global training is a good fit for you.
2. You decide if you're interested – if so, you sign up.
3. You work with a realtor in your area trained on how the system works.
4. You find a house and tell your realtor how much to offer.

5. Once the home is under contract to buy, you do your normal inspections and due diligence before closing. Throughout the process, you're making all the decisions because this is going to be your home. You decide what it's worth; you decide whether it's passing inspection. You have an option to back out by a certain date if it doesn't meet your standards just like any conventional purchase!

6. I arrange for a third party – an investor – to buy your house at the price you negotiated. This is a person who's familiar with the process, proven trustworthy, and has terrific credit.

7. The day the home closes, the house changes ownership to the investor (per the agreements you signed). You get to move in on the same day.

8. Soon after, when the documents have been prepared, the third party (who is now the owner) sells it to you and carries the mortgage as legally

prearranged. That's why I call it third-party owner financing!

The home is now in your name and you own it. You are now making your mortgage payments to a note servicing company that services the transaction for the life of the loan. You get the deed to your home of choice and immediately you start enjoying the benefits of home ownership!

The benefits to you?

- You now own the home that you chose.
- You never had to get your credit checked.
- You didn't get turned down simply for credit problems.
- You are free to create the memories you want in your own home, fix up your home, and change anything you want to change. It belongs to you.

The benefits to the home seller?

The original owner got what they wanted. They got to sell their home and walk off with whatever equity they had. They don't need to worry about getting paid because the third-party owner cashed them out already.

The benefits to the third-party owner?

They are getting cash flowing mortgage payments every month from you.

The benefit for TL Global?

We receive the training/mentoring fee and get to enjoy knowing that we helped others work together to create a win-win for everyone.

As I have said, I have been doing this since 2006. I've done well in multiple businesses, but never have I enjoyed creating a system this much. The amazing stories I'm hearing and seeing from my customers makes all my past struggles worthwhile.

When people have the money saved up for the down payment, that tells me that they're smart and determined. I don't worry about them making payments. I have hundreds of success stories to remind me just how easy this is.

I continue to monitor each case just to make sure everyone stays happy, and when I need to, I help resolve anything that comes up.

Is This for Real?

TL Global was organically grown as a mom-and-pop company. We've got good momentum, but if a person is not a good fit for our program, we let them know and let them go. We cannot succeed if we set you or anyone else up for failure.

Once we see you're a good fit, you can get an offer on third-party owner financing as soon as the next day.

Chapter 4:
Self-Evaluation Questionnaire

The home buyer in this system would still have a mortgage but would just pay it to a person instead of a bank. The advantage is the training and built-in systems to safeguard everyone in the agreements. If you were a lender, what safeguards would you like to have? What about the investor? The homebuyer?

Why is it important to have a disinterested note servicing company involved to take the monthly payments? How does it help avoid disagreements between the buyer and investor?

How do you know if you're a good fit for owner financing? Do you have adequate income? Down payment? Are you able to get a bank loan?

In this system, all parties get something they want, whether the buyer, seller, real estate agent, investor, or others on the team. To preserve peace, all documents are clear, and training provided. There is also a team available to help get through any struggles. At what point in the sale do you move into your new home?

CHAPTER 5

MAKING IT EASY

Okay. Now you're probably wondering, "How can you say it's simple and easy when there are so many people involved?" Glad you asked!

The reason it's simple and easy for you is that all these professionals have set up a framework to get third-party owner financing for you in a safe, easy, and effective way.

Believe me, it wasn't easy in the beginning because we were building the plane while we were flying it. It wasn't organized into a business. We just wanted our loved ones to be able to buy homes when it looked impossible. But as time went by and we found out how many we could help, it just felt better and better to smooth out all the wrinkles in the plan.

We brainstormed for years to work out the nuts and bolts of the system, sharing notes and fine-tuning as we went. I now believe that I have the most successful mentoring system in the world for third-party owner financing, and I'm proud to share it with you and others.

I asked some people who experienced this process to share their stories for the book. Here is what they relayed to my team for you.

Keith

"I worked hard all the time, but I had no credit. It was hard trying to get a house. Some people want that dream home, and I did. I went through a lot before we heard of the TL Global class and went down and signed up. I had no idea what a huge change it would make in my life. I finally scored my dream and even more than a house.

"They made it easy. They do everything! They thought of everything. This is a nice organization; they're friendly, warm, and genuine. They even help you get your electricity started and a cable company. When I got the house, they were there to give me the keys.

"They do everything – residential and industrial. I wanted to start a detail pressure-washing business, and they helped me get a building for that. I started wanting to get a house to rent out, and they made sure I got that, too.

"And I kept reaching out. I got a mentor from them. Once you sign up with them, they'll work with you, and you can call for anything. There's no charge – they'll hear you out. They'll brainstorm for a week or two until they find an answer for you – a plan that works."

Keith worked hard to save for a house, and he understands why some people are afraid to try the program. He explained, "People work hard to save and get houses. They're afraid of losing their tuition money. They won't even take the walk to see where it leads. But these people, they make sure you don't lose."

He started referring other people to TL Global. "I'm not a realtor, but I knew people who had saved money for a home, so I referred them. Then, I'd see them enroll in the class and get a big home.

"TL Global is a nice family. They help you get further in life. They were right there for me.

"I've been through a lot, and I've been with them for two years now. For me, the mentoring was a good decision. They're a good organization."

Cindy

"My husband and I were both divorced; therefore, our credit wasn't the best. As newlyweds, we wanted our own home. The owner of the house we were renting did not want to sell to us, so that's when we decided to hunt for another home.

"We got a real estate agent and went through the traditional lending process, which denied our application until we could fix our damaged credit. But even then, there was no guarantee that we could qualify.

"We got an email advertisement about TL Global, and then we met with Shaker and his team to get the process going. The process was painless!"

Shaker and his team were great in answering all our questions and working with us. We are happy with our purchase and would recommend this program to anyone who finds themselves on the outside looking in. We are happy to say this: We're are the proud owners of a home we can call our own."

Emily

In 2016, Emily and her husband were living in Houston and had a new baby, their first. Emily's mother-in-law lived with them. They always wanted to move to Denver if the opportunity ever came up, and in 2017, they got the chance. They all moved together. After a while, Grandma decided to move back to Houston, and she did.

Before too long, they realized that the high elevation in Denver wasn't a good fit for their little girl. She had croup, apparently caused by the thin air. She was sick all the time. The croup got so bad that they had to take her to the emergency room five times within four months. They realized that they could travel anytime and fly from anywhere, but they needed to move back to Houston.

They moved back to Houston and leased a beautiful high rise. But with a toddler, it wasn't enough. It was a home, but not a forever home. After three years, as their lease renewal was coming up, they knew they didn't want to lease for another year. They wanted stability for their daughter and needed to figure out a way to move into a new home.

They knew what they wanted in a home but modified their criteria a bit when Grandma expressed an interest in moving back in with them. They knew they would figure out a way.

Emily, an accountant, had been to the TL Global training before and had kept in touch. They were looking for new construction and they knew the neighborhood and builder they wanted. They had done their research.

They found a home they liked, but the builder had already accepted an offer. They looked at several more and found one – but it was already in escrow. At the last minute, the buyers' loan didn't go through! The house fell out of escrow on March 15, 2020.

Til and Emily jumped into action. In short order, the third-party owner financing was set, and they closed on their new home in just fifteen days – on April 1.

Grandma moved in within two weeks and accepted an offer on her own home, which was now in escrow.

The little girl is almost four years old now and much healthier. She loves the house and loves having Grandma around! There are kids in the neighborhood to play with and a nice park nearby. Most of all, the home provides stability.

Emily says, "My experience was great. I clicked with Til and she clicked with me. We understood what each other wanted and worked well together. She cared and wanted my family to be healthy and safe. Her team was great, too. They were always upfront, honest, and transparent. There's a cost, and if you understand that, everything else is great. I never had the feeling that something wasn't right."

Mary

Mary, a generous individual, didn't have a high enough credit score to buy a home. She had cosigned loans to help a few relatives buy cars, and they defaulted. She didn't think it was right to pay off their loans, so she didn't, and her credit score suffered as a result.

When she retired, she knew that she couldn't survive on retirement and Social Security alone. Besides, she needed a house to start a home business. She also knew that money sitting idle tends to filter away.

She had cash saved up and started looking at houses. Even though she had a $40,000 down payment, she couldn't get a bank loan. So, she started looking at homes with owner financing.

One day, she saw a sign in front of a house that said, "Special Financing." She thought, "What the heck? I might as well call and see what it's all about." She did, and met Richard, the real estate agent. He explained about

Til and how she started and grew her financing business. Richard listened to Mary's situation and how she wanted to work at home. He thought she was a good candidate for TL Global and taught her the process.

Mary started the paperwork process and qualified! She was so happy and relieved!

Richard guided her through the process, and it was hassle-free. She never even had to meet with the investor. Richard sent her to an attorney's office to sign the papers, and she was able to move in and start her home business immediately.

But what was this home business she was so keen on starting? Mary had been fostering dogs from rescues. She was such a great foster mom that the rescue volunteers always asked her if she could take more. They even told her, "We'll pay you!"

As it turned out, not only was Mary lucky to find financing for the home, but she's now happily fostering some really lucky dogs.

As she puts it, "It has worked out wonderfully."

Carol

Carol didn't want to live in an apartment forever, but being self-employed, her income was sometimes up, sometimes down, and sometimes, she even lost money! Her credit was very good, but institutional lenders always wanted to see two years of tax returns and stable income. She couldn't show that.

She had savings for a down payment, so she started looking online. Then, she saw a website that advertised: "We don't check your credit, income, or anything."

"Wow!" she thought. "They don't check your income! I'll give it a try."

Shortly, she met Barry, who explained the program, and she went to a presentation. About two months later, she moved into her own place. The cost was higher due to a higher interest rate, but no other lender could do it.

She started making payments and all went well for a while. She got a fulltime, stable job. After about a year, she could show the stable income and decided to refinance with a traditional lender.

She called several places and found an institutional mortgage broker that would work with her. The refinance finally went through, the payments got much lower, and life got easier. She started a new phase of her life.

TL Global helped Carol when she had no other choice. It wasn't too complicated, and there wasn't any trouble with it. She's had her refinanced loan for about a year now and is doing well.

It's Your Choice

When I talk to people, I don't tell them what to decide. I show them what avenues to consider.

As you can see, lots of people have problems with credit, but that doesn't mean they shouldn't own a home. We believe that every family who has saved up for a home deserves to get one of their choice —no matter what their credit situation is.

Banks don't want to take any risks on people, but that doesn't mean that the people don't deserve a home.

Chapter 5:
Self-Evaluation Questionnaire

As you heard in the stories, people can have bad credit even if they are highly responsible and have a down payment saved up. Do you know of anyone dreaming of home ownership who can't get a bank loan?

You read the story of Carol, who was single but wanted her own home. The longer she stayed in the apartment, the longer her chances of building up equity slipped away. There is a fee for the training and the interest rate is high enough to satisfy the investor. Can you see Carol's logic in getting into a home sooner than later?

Can you relate to the case studies or know anyone in one of those positions?

When you think of your own life, is it important to own a home for financial or any other reason?

CHAPTER 6

STEERING THROUGH THE
ROUGH WATERS

By now, you might be wondering what is taken into consideration when looking for a good fit.

- First, your cash is your credit. If you have the money to buy a house and problems getting a conventional loan, I can help you get third-party financing.

- Secondly, I meet with you in person, the old-fashioned way, to make sure you understand

everything and that we are a good fit for each
other.

- Third, my plan is to make sure you get
  competitive terms given your current situation.
  My model is not good for people who can get a
  low-rate bank loan on their own.

A lot of people don't like taking the risk of committing to
buying a home though. That decision is not mine to make
on behalf of other people. Everyone is entitled to decide
what is best for them and their family. While some are
risk-tolerant and some are risk-averse, each should be
respected in the same way, and neither should take on a
risk that they cannot afford if things ever went wrong.

I make three promises to anyone I work with:

1. I'll be with you throughout the whole process and
   have your best interest in mind.
2. It will not be scary.
3. There is no guilt whatever you decide.

Chapter 6:
Self-Evaluation Questionnaire

Do you fall into the category of needing a loan, having enough money to buy a home, but not being able to get one through the usual channels?

With me, there are no surprises, but I only work with people who understand the process. Are you able to envision how the process works? It's not for everybody, but people who have a large down payment and a steady income but unable to get a bank loan are the best fits for what I do.

When my dad decided to put us in a boat and take a chance on a new life, he took us to a world where we could have more than we ever dreamed of. Are you open to new ideas to help you achieve your dream?

I have always wanted to give back to America since we moved here and started over. I'll never forget peeling shrimp for long days for pennies in America. The difference is that here, people can pull themselves out of a dead-end job and reroute their lives. I hope that in this book, I have rerouted your discouragement into hope.

CHAPTER 7

WHAT TO EXPECT

In case you're wondering if you would be a good fit for my mentoring, I want to give you an idea of how a typical meeting would go. Let's imagine that we're meeting face to face.

1. Day 1: Welcome. We meet face to face at a prearranged place and time, usually in my office in Houston, Texas.
2. We talk and exchange information about what kind of home you want and what your situation is.

3. I explain the nuts and bolts of exactly how a person gets a home through third-party owner financing. By the end of our meeting, you understand all the ins and outs of how it works.

4. You take some time to decide on whether this method appeals to you. If I am aware of more beneficial options for you elsewhere, I will let you know that there is a better way.

5. If you like everything you hear, you are welcomed into the program to sign up for mentoring, and you pay a training fee. This means you'll be guided every step of the way until you get your dream home!

6. You will start looking at homes with a trained realtor familiar with the third-party owner financing process.

7. When you find the right house, you tell the realtor how much you want to offer on the house. If the offer is accepted, you execute the contract by paying a small option fee and a small amount of

earnest money, which creates legal agreements that protect you. This gives you a little bit of time to do due diligence and decide if you want to move forward.

8. Now, it's time for you to inspect the home to make sure you know the condition of the house and that there are no surprises. You pick any inspector you want. Their job is to point out every defect they find so you can make an informed decision, or even renegotiate with the seller!

9. Once you approve the condition and price of the home as-is and would like to move forward, it is time to commit.

10. We'll go through all the necessary documentation and agreements together in detail, so you know exactly what you're agreeing to and what the other parties are agreeing to. This means that every party meets their end of the deal.

11. At this point, you place additional earnest money in order to show you are totally serious about

moving forward. An investor is assigned to purchase the house for you, and everything else is taken care of. It becomes a short waiting game while the investor provides everything the bank needs to see and secures the financing,

12. When the contract closes, the seller is cashed out, the title is transferred, the realtor gets a commission, and you get the keys to move in on the same day!

13. Meanwhile, the home is in the name of the investor. You wait a short period of time for the real estate attorney to draw up the documents to record the deed in your name. (This was specified in the owner financing agreement.)

14. You schedule a time to sit down with the attorney to review all the paperwork and agreements. He/she acts as a neutral third party that explains every document in detail, making sure you feel secure because you know the kinds of safeguards built into the agreements to protect your interest.

15. The house is now yours and you make the mortgage payments to a third-party note servicing company, which ensures you have peace of mind knowing your investment is secure.

Everyone is happy – the seller, the realtor, the title company, and the third-party owner-financer. Most of all, you are because you can finally enjoy the benefits of home ownership!

I've mentored hundreds of happy clients. When you work with that many people, there will inevitably be a few unhappy ones due to outside circumstances, but I do my best to be a problem solver. I think that's my special talent and why I love doing this job the way I do.

I had a client once who got into the house and made all her mortgage payments for a while, but suddenly, something really sad happened. She got divorced, and she couldn't pay. I stretched out her agreement and made exceptions long past the time most people would have foreclosed on her, but eventually, it had to happen. There was nothing I could do.

Then, I had an idea.

I realized that her house was going to need cleaning after she moved out so it could be shown to potential buyers.

I called her up, allowed her to stay until the home sold, and offered her a cleaning job. She accepted, tidied the house up for pay, and showed the home until it was sold. She still works for me to this day, cleaning houses to get them show-ready.

Instead of booting her out, leaving the home in bad condition, and trying to fire-sale the property, it ended up working out for both of us. She had more time to figure out moving arrangements, made some money, and gained a part time gig going forward. It was a win/win.

It's situations like this that make my life worthwhile. I love finding unique and creative solutions to the many problems that come up in the real estate business. I have a lot of experience in it, and I realize that the best way to get ahead is to treat people fairly.

Chapter 7:
Self-Evaluation Questionnaire

1. In this method of getting a loan, who picks out the house?

    A. You

    B. The lender

    C. Me

2. When you have chosen the house you want, the price you offer the seller is decided by:

    A. The realtor

    B. The seller's agent

    C. You.

3. While you're in escrow, who arranges the due diligence (inspections) to make sure the house is sound?

    A. You – it's your house so you want to make sure it's in acceptable condition.

    B. Nobody – you just hope it's good.

    C. A long-lost relative

4. When you get the keys, how long do you have to wait to get the house in your name?

    A. It's almost immediate but might take a few days.

    B. 60 days

    C. 6 years

Answers:

1. You

2. You

CHAPTER 8

MY "WHY"

Why do I do this? Why did I stick with this business for so many years even though it required years of groundwork to get it right?

That might be one of the questions going through your mind.

It's because at one time, I needed help getting a home but didn't want to ask. It was literally impossible for me to get a home, but in fact, I couldn't even get an apartment in my name! Fortunately, I had a friend who helped me.

I was so grateful that I had that friend. But I thought to myself that there must be so many "me's" floating around! So many that don't have a friend like that.

It became my mission to help all the other "me's" out there.

People make money doing bad things or good things. I choose good. This business and all the brain power that went into it is by far my pride and joy. It makes me feel good when I see other people so happy because they got a home when no one else would help them.

If your hard-earned money can't buy you what you want, what good is your hard-earned money?

Dream big. Learn. Grab your dreams. It's all about the memories you're going to create.

"Great businesses are not built by extraordinary people but by ordinary people doing extraordinary things."

Michael Gerber
Author, The E-Myth

Chapter 8: Self Evaluation Questionnaire

It was my dream to pay America back for all the opportunity. Do you dream big? Have past experiences dragged you down?

I had to wrack my brain and think through this whole process until it was foolproof. Are you ready to rethink your experiences and start new?

Like my dad, sometimes I had to reach deep into myself to keep going at times. But I promise it won't be scary. Are you a go-getter that doesn't mind working hard to get what you want?

I make three promises to everyone who works with me: (1) you'll never be alone – I'll be with you the whole time until the day I place your key into your hand. (2) It won't be scary. (3) There is no guilt whatever you decide. Does this sound appealing to you?

CHAPTER 9

TRANSPARENCY

When I meet with homebuyers, I always do it one-on-one to maintain confidentiality. When I train realtors or investors, I do it in groups. Before I work with anybody, I want to make sure they understand third-party owner financing.

Everything is systematized. I like it better that way. No surprises.

I give copies of the paperwork to everybody. It's designed to protect all the parties involved. If anyone in the system doesn't perform, the safeguards protect that person and the others – because if you work with me, I want to protect everyone. Even if you find that you can't make payments, we can protect your credit. That's because you have choices built in.

It's all about teamwork and transparency. Everyone has an area of expertise. Every transaction is a win/win/win.

I've worked for years with my attorneys to not only make sure everything's legal, but to nail down all the variables. We studied, got input, and tested all the pieces of the puzzle ever since the first time I helped the first person 14 years ago. There's no stepping on each other's toes. That's the power of a team.

Zig Ziglar says that if you help others prosper, you will prosper as well. The homebuyer helps the third-party owner and vice-versa. Everyone gets what they need and want – the homebuyer, title company, insurance company, Realtor, appraiser, coach, investor, etc. We all have support each step of the way.

Some of my clients are so happy that they refer friends to me. After all, they know all the pros of owning vs. renting:

1. You get to write off the interest you pay on your mortgage (see your accountant, of course).
2. You get the joy of owning your own home.
3. You have the freedom to fix it up, remodel, paint, plant, etc. No landlord to consult!
4. You can rent out a room if you want.
5. You can have as many pets as you want (within the law).
6. You will build memories. This is the best part. As you look around your home, your memories of the love and good times linger on. It's a great comfort and joy.

That's what I would love to see for everyone, and that's why I work so hard at doing it.

Chapter 9:
Self-Evaluation Questionnaire

Why is it important to protect all parties in a transaction?

How can using third-party owner financing help protect your credit when a bank won't?

Why was working with attorneys and brainstorming over a number of years so important when trying to protect all parties?

What are the pros and cons of owning vs. renting?

FREQUENTLY ASKED QUESTIONS

What is owner financing?

Owner financing is when the buyer seeks financing directly from the person selling a property. In third-party owner financing, this person will be a real estate investor.

What if I have bad credit? Can I still get a home with owner financing?

Yes, you can! Every situation is different, but we specialize in helping people who have been through tough circumstances (or just made mistakes in the past) to get started on the path to a great financial future and home ownership.

What are the benefits of owner financing?

There are a lot of benefits to owner financing! Lots of smart people are using owner financing as a way to get the home of their dreams without having to qualify for a bank loan. In the past few years, banks have been very tight on their lending criteria, making it harder for people to purchase homes.

All the banks have turned down my mortgage application. Can you still help me buy a home?

This program has been founded with the sole purpose of helping individuals and families who can't qualify for a conventional mortgage. We have helped hundreds of families realize their home ownership dream even when everyone else has told them, "No."

How do I get started?

Fill out the form at www.GetOwnerFinancing.com. Once you submit the form, you will be directed to schedule an appointment for a live meeting with us.

What happens at the face-to-face meeting at your offices in Houston?

We take you through all the details of our program and explain exactly how we can get you any house you want with no credit check and no income check. We also get to know about you and your situation. We give you full disclosure and expect honesty in return. If everything matches up, we can move forward.

Can I refinance at any time?

Yes, there is no pre-payment penalty, so as soon as your finances and/or credit are back on track, you can refinance into a traditional bank mortgage.

Contact Us

I bet there are still questions for you that I haven't answered. To learn more, you can always contact us here:

GetOwnerFinancing.com
ShopOwnerFinance.com
Office: 1 (713) 382-5000
Email: wecare@getownerfinancing.com

Last, I'd just like to thank you for reading this book. And, thank Andrea Robinson for helping me bring this book to life for you. If there are any comments or anything you would like me to include in the next edition, please let me know. If you'd like to order a book for a friend, just ask. We'll be more than happy to send one to them.

Happy home owning!

Til

Made in the USA
Middletown, DE
05 April 2022

63602897R00056